INFORMATION

MW01377734

BUSINESS NAME	
Registration Details	
Address:	
Phone No.		Email	
Fax No.		Emergency No.	
Website	
Log Book Number	
Continued From Log Book:		Continued To Log Book:	
Date Log Started:		Date Log Ended:	

NOTES

_____
_____
_____
_____
_____
_____
_____
_____
_____
_____

www.signatureplannerjournals.com
www.signatureplannerjournals.co.uk

CONTENTS

Livestock Record Log ....Page 2-31

Equipment Inventory Log .... Page 32-37

Equipment Repair Log... Page 38-57

Farm Expense Record .... Page 58-77

Farm Income Record ....Page 78-97

Notes .... Page 98-107

Calendars..Page 108

LIVESTOCK RECORD

		Start Date:			End of Year:			
#	TYPE OF LIVESTOCK	QTY	AVG. WEIGHT	VALUE	QTY	AVG. WEIGHT	VALUE	BALANCE

Year: _____

LIVESTOCK RECORD

Year:		Start Date:			End of Year:			
#	TYPE OF LIVESTOCK	QTY	AVG. WEIGHT	VALUE	QTY	AVG. WEIGHT	VALUE	BALANCE

LIVESTOCK RECORD

Year:		Start Date:			End of Year:			
#	TYPE OF LIVESTOCK	QTY	AVG. WEIGHT	VALUE	QTY	AVG. WEIGHT	VALUE	BALANCE

LIVESTOCK RECORD

Year:		Start Date:			End of Year:			
#	TYPE OF LIVESTOCK	QTY	AVG. WEIGHT	VALUE	QTY	AVG. WEIGHT	VALUE	BALANCE

LIVESTOCK RECORD

Year:		Start Date:			End of Year:			
#	TYPE OF LIVESTOCK	QTY	AVG. WEIGHT	VALUE	QTY	AVG. WEIGHT	VALUE	BALANCE

LIVESTOCK RECORD

Year:		Start Date:			End of Year:			
#	TYPE OF LIVESTOCK	QTY	AVG. WEIGHT	VALUE	QTY	AVG. WEIGHT	VALUE	BALANCE

LIVESTOCK RECORD

Year:		Start Date:			End of Year:			
#	TYPE OF LIVESTOCK	QTY	AVG. WEIGHT	VALUE	QTY	AVG. WEIGHT	VALUE	BALANCE

LIVESTOCK RECORD

Year:		Start Date:			End of Year:			
#	TYPE OF LIVESTOCK	QTY	AVG. WEIGHT	VALUE	QTY	AVG. WEIGHT	VALUE	BALANCE

LIVESTOCK RECORD

Year:		Start Date:			End of Year:			
#	TYPE OF LIVESTOCK	QTY	AVG. WEIGHT	VALUE	QTY	AVG. WEIGHT	VALUE	BALANCE

LIVESTOCK RECORD

Year:		Start Date:			End of Year:			
#	TYPE OF LIVESTOCK	QTY	AVG. WEIGHT	VALUE	QTY	AVG. WEIGHT	VALUE	BALANCE

LIVESTOCK RECORD

Year:		Start Date:			End of Year:			
#	TYPE OF LIVESTOCK	QTY	AVG. WEIGHT	VALUE	QTY	AVG. WEIGHT	VALUE	BALANCE

LIVESTOCK RECORD

Year:		Start Date:			End of Year:			
#	TYPE OF LIVESTOCK	QTY	AVG. WEIGHT	VALUE	QTY	AVG. WEIGHT	VALUE	BALANCE

LIVESTOCK RECORD

Year:		Start Date:			End of Year:			
#	TYPE OF LIVESTOCK	QTY	AVG. WEIGHT	VALUE	QTY	AVG. WEIGHT	VALUE	BALANCE

LIVESTOCK RECORD

Year:		Start Date:			End of Year:			
#	TYPE OF LIVESTOCK	QTY	AVG. WEIGHT	VALUE	QTY	AVG. WEIGHT	VALUE	BALANCE

LIVESTOCK RECORD

Year:		Start Date:			End of Year:			
#	TYPE OF LIVESTOCK	QTY	AVG. WEIGHT	VALUE	QTY	AVG. WEIGHT	VALUE	BALANCE

LIVESTOCK RECORD

Year:		Start Date:			End of Year:			
#	TYPE OF LIVESTOCK	QTY	AVG. WEIGHT	VALUE	QTY	AVG. WEIGHT	VALUE	BALANCE

LIVESTOCK RECORD

Year:		Start Date:			End of Year:			
#	TYPE OF LIVESTOCK	QTY	AVG. WEIGHT	VALUE	QTY	AVG. WEIGHT	VALUE	BALANCE

LIVESTOCK RECORD

Year:		Start Date:			End of Year:			
#	TYPE OF LIVESTOCK	QTY	AVG. WEIGHT	VALUE	QTY	AVG. WEIGHT	VALUE	BALANCE

LIVESTOCK RECORD

Year:		Start Date:			End of Year:			
#	TYPE OF LIVESTOCK	QTY	AVG. WEIGHT	VALUE	QTY	AVG. WEIGHT	VALUE	BALANCE

LIVESTOCK RECORD

Year:		Start Date:			End of Year:			
#	TYPE OF LIVESTOCK	QTY	AVG. WEIGHT	VALUE	QTY	AVG. WEIGHT	VALUE	BALANCE

LIVESTOCK RECORD

Year:		Start Date:			End of Year:			
#	TYPE OF LIVESTOCK	QTY	AVG. WEIGHT	VALUE	QTY	AVG. WEIGHT	VALUE	BALANCE

LIVESTOCK RECORD

Year:		Start Date:			End of Year:			
#	TYPE OF LIVESTOCK	QTY	AVG. WEIGHT	VALUE	QTY	AVG. WEIGHT	VALUE	BALANCE

LIVESTOCK RECORD

Year:		Start Date:			End of Year:			
#	TYPE OF LIVESTOCK	QTY	AVG. WEIGHT	VALUE	QTY	AVG. WEIGHT	VALUE	BALANCE

LIVESTOCK RECORD

Year:		Start Date:			End of Year:			
#	TYPE OF LIVESTOCK	QTY	AVG. WEIGHT	VALUE	QTY	AVG. WEIGHT	VALUE	BALANCE

LIVESTOCK RECORD

Year:		Start Date:			End of Year:			
#	TYPE OF LIVESTOCK	QTY	AVG. WEIGHT	VALUE	QTY	AVG. WEIGHT	VALUE	BALANCE

LIVESTOCK RECORD

Year:		Start Date:			End of Year:			
#	TYPE OF LIVESTOCK	QTY	AVG. WEIGHT	VALUE	QTY	AVG. WEIGHT	VALUE	BALANCE

LIVESTOCK RECORD

Year:		Start Date:			End of Year:			
#	TYPE OF LIVESTOCK	QTY	AVG. WEIGHT	VALUE	QTY	AVG. WEIGHT	VALUE	BALANCE

LIVESTOCK RECORD

Year:		Start Date:			End of Year:			
#	TYPE OF LIVESTOCK	QTY	AVG. WEIGHT	VALUE	QTY	AVG. WEIGHT	VALUE	BALANCE

LIVESTOCK RECORD

Year:		Start Date:			End of Year:			
#	TYPE OF LIVESTOCK	QTY	AVG. WEIGHT	VALUE	QTY	AVG. WEIGHT	VALUE	BALANCE

LIVESTOCK RECORD

Year:		Start Date:			End of Year:			
#	TYPE OF LIVESTOCK	QTY	AVG. WEIGHT	VALUE	QTY	AVG. WEIGHT	VALUE	BALANCE

EQUIPMENT INVENTORY

#	LOCATION	ITEM DESCRIPTION	SERIAL NO.	MODEL	PURCHASE DATE	COST
1						
2						
3						
4						
5						
6						
7						
8						
9						
10						
11						
12						
13						
14						
15						
16						
17						
18						
19						
20						
21						
22						
23						
24						
25						
26						
27						
28						
29						
30						

EQUIPMENT INVENTORY

#	LOCATION	ITEM DESCRIPTION	SERIAL NO.	MODEL	PURCHASE DATE	COST
31						
32						
33						
34						
35						
36						
37						
38						
39						
40						
41						
42						
43						
44						
45						
46						
47						
48						
49						
50						
51						
52						
53						
54						
55						
56						
57						
58						
59						
60						

EQUIPMENT INVENTORY

#	LOCATION	ITEM DESCRIPTION	SERIAL NO.	MODEL	PURCHASE DATE	COST
61						
62						
63						
64						
65						
66						
67						
68						
69						
70						
71						
72						
73						
74						
75						
76						
77						
78						
79						
80						
81						
82						
83						
84						
85						
86						
87						
88						
89						
90						

EQUIPMENT INVENTORY

#	LOCATION	ITEM DESCRIPTION	SERIAL NO.	MODEL	PURCHASE DATE	COST
91						
92						
93						
94						
95						
96						
97						
98						
99						
100						
101						
102						
103						
104						
105						
106						
107						
108						
109						
110						
111						
112						
113						
114						
115						
116						
117						
118						
119						
120						

EQUIPMENT INVENTORY

#	LOCATION	ITEM DESCRIPTION	SERIAL NO.	MODEL	PURCHASE DATE	COST

EQUIPMENT INVENTORY

#	LOCATION	ITEM DESCRIPTION	SERIAL NO.	MODEL	PURCHASE DATE	COST

EQUIPMENT REPAIR LOG

Date		Equipment	
Serial No.		Model	
Repair Reason			

REPAIR DETAILS/ COST

Repaired by		**Warranty**	
Parts Replaced		YES	NO

Date		Equipment	
Serial No.		Model	
Repair Reason			

REPAIR DETAILS/ COST

Repaired by		**Warranty**	
Parts Replaced		YES	NO

Date		Equipment	
Serial No.		Model	
Repair Reason			

REPAIR DETAILS/ COST

Repaired by		**Warranty**	
Parts Replaced		YES	NO

Date		Equipment	
Serial No.		Model	
Repair Reason			

REPAIR DETAILS/ COST

Repaired by		**Warranty**	
Parts Replaced		YES	NO

EQUIPMENT REPAIR LOG

Date		Equipment		
Serial No.		Model		
Repair Reason				

REPAIR DETAILS/ COST		

Repaired by		**Warranty**	
Parts Replaced		YES	NO

Date		Equipment		
Serial No.		Model		
Repair Reason				

REPAIR DETAILS/ COST		

Repaired by		**Warranty**	
Parts Replaced		YES	NO

Date		Equipment		
Serial No.		Model		
Repair Reason				

REPAIR DETAILS/ COST		

Repaired by		**Warranty**	
Parts Replaced		YES	NO

Date		Equipment		
Serial No.		Model		
Repair Reason				

REPAIR DETAILS/ COST		

Repaired by		**Warranty**	
Parts Replaced		YES	NO

EQUIPMENT REPAIR LOG

Date		Equipment	
Serial No.		Model	
Repair Reason			

REPAIR DETAILS/ COST

| | |
| | |

| Repaired by | | **Warranty** | |
| Parts Replaced | | YES | NO |

Date		Equipment	
Serial No.		Model	
Repair Reason			

REPAIR DETAILS/ COST

| | |
| | |

| Repaired by | | **Warranty** | |
| Parts Replaced | | YES | NO |

Date		Equipment	
Serial No.		Model	
Repair Reason			

REPAIR DETAILS/ COST

| | |
| | |

| Repaired by | | **Warranty** | |
| Parts Replaced | | YES | NO |

Date		Equipment	
Serial No.		Model	
Repair Reason			

REPAIR DETAILS/ COST

| | |
| | |

| Repaired by | | **Warranty** | |
| Parts Replaced | | YES | NO |

EQUIPMENT REPAIR LOG

Date		Equipment		
Serial No.		Model		
Repair Reason				

REPAIR DETAILS/ COST

Repaired by			**Warranty**	
Parts Replaced			YES	NO

Date		Equipment		
Serial No.		Model		
Repair Reason				

REPAIR DETAILS/ COST

Repaired by			**Warranty**	
Parts Replaced			YES	NO

Date		Equipment		
Serial No.		Model		
Repair Reason				

REPAIR DETAILS/ COST

Repaired by			**Warranty**	
Parts Replaced			YES	NO

Date		Equipment		
Serial No.		Model		
Repair Reason				

REPAIR DETAILS/ COST

Repaired by			**Warranty**	
Parts Replaced			YES	NO

EQUIPMENT REPAIR LOG

Date		Equipment	
Serial No.		Model	
Repair Reason			

REPAIR DETAILS/ COST

Repaired by			Warranty	
Parts Replaced			YES	NO

Date		Equipment	
Serial No.		Model	
Repair Reason			

REPAIR DETAILS/ COST

Repaired by			Warranty	
Parts Replaced			YES	NO

Date		Equipment	
Serial No.		Model	
Repair Reason			

REPAIR DETAILS/ COST

Repaired by			Warranty	
Parts Replaced			YES	NO

Date		Equipment	
Serial No.		Model	
Repair Reason			

REPAIR DETAILS/ COST

Repaired by			Warranty	
Parts Replaced			YES	NO

EQUIPMENT REPAIR LOG

Date		Equipment		
Serial No.		Model		
Repair Reason				

REPAIR DETAILS/ COST

Repaired by		**Warranty**	
Parts Replaced		YES	NO

Date		Equipment		
Serial No.		Model		
Repair Reason				

REPAIR DETAILS/ COST

Repaired by		**Warranty**	
Parts Replaced		YES	NO

Date		Equipment		
Serial No.		Model		
Repair Reason				

REPAIR DETAILS/ COST

Repaired by		**Warranty**	
Parts Replaced		YES	NO

Date		Equipment		
Serial No.		Model		
Repair Reason				

REPAIR DETAILS/ COST

Repaired by		**Warranty**	
Parts Replaced		YES	NO

EQUIPMENT REPAIR LOG

Date		Equipment	
Serial No.		Model	
Repair Reason			

REPAIR DETAILS/ COST

Repaired by			**Warranty**	
Parts Replaced			YES	NO

Date		Equipment	
Serial No.		Model	
Repair Reason			

REPAIR DETAILS/ COST

Repaired by			**Warranty**	
Parts Replaced			YES	NO

Date		Equipment	
Serial No.		Model	
Repair Reason			

REPAIR DETAILS/ COST

Repaired by			**Warranty**	
Parts Replaced			YES	NO

Date		Equipment	
Serial No.		Model	
Repair Reason			

REPAIR DETAILS/ COST

Repaired by			**Warranty**	
Parts Replaced			YES	NO

EQUIPMENT REPAIR LOG

Date		Equipment		
Serial No.		Model		
Repair Reason				

REPAIR DETAILS/ COST

Repaired by		**Warranty**	
Parts Replaced		YES	NO

Date		Equipment		
Serial No.		Model		
Repair Reason				

REPAIR DETAILS/ COST

Repaired by		**Warranty**	
Parts Replaced		YES	NO

Date		Equipment		
Serial No.		Model		
Repair Reason				

REPAIR DETAILS/ COST

Repaired by		**Warranty**	
Parts Replaced		YES	NO

Date		Equipment		
Serial No.		Model		
Repair Reason				

REPAIR DETAILS/ COST

Repaired by		**Warranty**	
Parts Replaced		YES	NO

EQUIPMENT REPAIR LOG

Date		Equipment	
Serial No.		Model	
Repair Reason			

REPAIR DETAILS/ COST

Repaired by		**Warranty**	
Parts Replaced		YES	NO

Date		Equipment	
Serial No.		Model	
Repair Reason			

REPAIR DETAILS/ COST

Repaired by		**Warranty**	
Parts Replaced		YES	NO

Date		Equipment	
Serial No.		Model	
Repair Reason			

REPAIR DETAILS/ COST

Repaired by		**Warranty**	
Parts Replaced		YES	NO

Date		Equipment	
Serial No.		Model	
Repair Reason			

REPAIR DETAILS/ COST

Repaired by		**Warranty**	
Parts Replaced		YES	NO

EQUIPMENT REPAIR LOG

Date		Equipment	
Serial No.		Model	
Repair Reason			

REPAIR DETAILS/ COST		

Repaired by		Warranty	
Parts Replaced		YES	NO

Date		Equipment	
Serial No.		Model	
Repair Reason			

REPAIR DETAILS/ COST		

Repaired by		Warranty	
Parts Replaced		YES	NO

Date		Equipment	
Serial No.		Model	
Repair Reason			

REPAIR DETAILS/ COST		

Repaired by		Warranty	
Parts Replaced		YES	NO

Date		Equipment	
Serial No.		Model	
Repair Reason			

REPAIR DETAILS/ COST		

Repaired by		Warranty	
Parts Replaced		YES	NO

EQUIPMENT REPAIR LOG

Date		Equipment	
Serial No.		Model	
Repair Reason			

REPAIR DETAILS/ COST

Repaired by		**Warranty**	
Parts Replaced		YES	NO

Date		Equipment	
Serial No.		Model	
Repair Reason			

REPAIR DETAILS/ COST

Repaired by		**Warranty**	
Parts Replaced		YES	NO

Date		Equipment	
Serial No.		Model	
Repair Reason			

REPAIR DETAILS/ COST

Repaired by		**Warranty**	
Parts Replaced		YES	NO

Date		Equipment	
Serial No.		Model	
Repair Reason			

REPAIR DETAILS/ COST

Repaired by		**Warranty**	
Parts Replaced		YES	NO

EQUIPMENT REPAIR LOG

Date		Equipment	
Serial No.		Model	
Repair Reason			

REPAIR DETAILS/ COST

Repaired by			**Warranty**	
Parts Replaced			YES	NO

Date		Equipment	
Serial No.		Model	
Repair Reason			

REPAIR DETAILS/ COST

Repaired by			**Warranty**	
Parts Replaced			YES	NO

Date		Equipment	
Serial No.		Model	
Repair Reason			

REPAIR DETAILS/ COST

Repaired by			**Warranty**	
Parts Replaced			YES	NO

Date		Equipment	
Serial No.		Model	
Repair Reason			

REPAIR DETAILS/ COST

Repaired by			**Warranty**	
Parts Replaced			YES	NO

EQUIPMENT REPAIR LOG

Date		Equipment	
Serial No.		Model	
Repair Reason			

REPAIR DETAILS/ COST

Repaired by			**Warranty**	
Parts Replaced			YES	NO

Date		Equipment	
Serial No.		Model	
Repair Reason			

REPAIR DETAILS/ COST

Repaired by			**Warranty**	
Parts Replaced			YES	NO

Date		Equipment	
Serial No.		Model	
Repair Reason			

REPAIR DETAILS/ COST

Repaired by			**Warranty**	
Parts Replaced			YES	NO

Date		Equipment	
Serial No.		Model	
Repair Reason			

REPAIR DETAILS/ COST

Repaired by			**Warranty**	
Parts Replaced			YES	NO

EQUIPMENT REPAIR LOG

Date		Equipment		
Serial No.		Model		
Repair Reason				

REPAIR DETAILS/ COST

		Warranty		
Repaired by				
Parts Replaced			YES	NO

Date		Equipment		
Serial No.		Model		
Repair Reason				

REPAIR DETAILS/ COST

		Warranty		
Repaired by				
Parts Replaced			YES	NO

Date		Equipment		
Serial No.		Model		
Repair Reason				

REPAIR DETAILS/ COST

		Warranty		
Repaired by				
Parts Replaced			YES	NO

Date		Equipment		
Serial No.		Model		
Repair Reason				

REPAIR DETAILS/ COST

		Warranty		
Repaired by				
Parts Replaced			YES	NO

EQUIPMENT REPAIR LOG

Date		Equipment	
Serial No.		Model	
Repair Reason			

REPAIR DETAILS/ COST

Repaired by		**Warranty**	
Parts Replaced		YES	NO

Date		Equipment	
Serial No.		Model	
Repair Reason			

REPAIR DETAILS/ COST

Repaired by		**Warranty**	
Parts Replaced		YES	NO

Date		Equipment	
Serial No.		Model	
Repair Reason			

REPAIR DETAILS/ COST

Repaired by		**Warranty**	
Parts Replaced		YES	NO

Date		Equipment	
Serial No.		Model	
Repair Reason			

REPAIR DETAILS/ COST

Repaired by		**Warranty**	
Parts Replaced		YES	NO

EQUIPMENT REPAIR LOG

Date		Equipment	
Serial No.		Model	
Repair Reason			

REPAIR DETAILS/ COST			

Repaired by		Warranty	
Parts Replaced		YES	NO

Date		Equipment	
Serial No.		Model	
Repair Reason			

REPAIR DETAILS/ COST			

Repaired by		Warranty	
Parts Replaced		YES	NO

Date		Equipment	
Serial No.		Model	
Repair Reason			

REPAIR DETAILS/ COST			

Repaired by		Warranty	
Parts Replaced		YES	NO

Date		Equipment	
Serial No.		Model	
Repair Reason			

REPAIR DETAILS/ COST			

Repaired by		Warranty	
Parts Replaced		YES	NO

EQUIPMENT REPAIR LOG

Date		Equipment	
Serial No.		Model	
Repair Reason			

REPAIR DETAILS/ COST

Repaired by		**Warranty**	
Parts Replaced		YES	NO

Date		Equipment	
Serial No.		Model	
Repair Reason			

REPAIR DETAILS/ COST

Repaired by		**Warranty**	
Parts Replaced		YES	NO

Date		Equipment	
Serial No.		Model	
Repair Reason			

REPAIR DETAILS/ COST

Repaired by		**Warranty**	
Parts Replaced		YES	NO

Date		Equipment	
Serial No.		Model	
Repair Reason			

REPAIR DETAILS/ COST

Repaired by		**Warranty**	
Parts Replaced		YES	NO

EQUIPMENT REPAIR LOG

Date		Equipment		
Serial No.		Model		
Repair Reason				

REPAIR DETAILS/ COST

Repaired by			**Warranty**	
Parts Replaced			YES	NO

Date		Equipment		
Serial No.		Model		
Repair Reason				

REPAIR DETAILS/ COST

Repaired by			**Warranty**	
Parts Replaced			YES	NO

Date		Equipment		
Serial No.		Model		
Repair Reason				

REPAIR DETAILS/ COST

Repaired by			**Warranty**	
Parts Replaced			YES	NO

Date		Equipment		
Serial No.		Model		
Repair Reason				

REPAIR DETAILS/ COST

Repaired by			**Warranty**	
Parts Replaced			YES	NO

EQUIPMENT REPAIR LOG

Date		Equipment	
Serial No.		Model	
Repair Reason			

REPAIR DETAILS/ COST

Repaired by		**Warranty**	
Parts Replaced		YES	NO

Date		Equipment	
Serial No.		Model	
Repair Reason			

REPAIR DETAILS/ COST

Repaired by		**Warranty**	
Parts Replaced		YES	NO

Date		Equipment	
Serial No.		Model	
Repair Reason			

REPAIR DETAILS/ COST

Repaired by		**Warranty**	
Parts Replaced		YES	NO

Date		Equipment	
Serial No.		Model	
Repair Reason			

REPAIR DETAILS/ COST

Repaired by		**Warranty**	
Parts Replaced		YES	NO

EQUIPMENT REPAIR LOG

Date		Equipment	
Serial No.		Model	
Repair Reason			

REPAIR DETAILS/ COST

Repaired by			**Warranty**	
Parts Replaced			YES	NO

Date		Equipment	
Serial No.		Model	
Repair Reason			

REPAIR DETAILS/ COST

Repaired by			**Warranty**	
Parts Replaced			YES	NO

Date		Equipment	
Serial No.		Model	
Repair Reason			

REPAIR DETAILS/ COST

Repaired by			**Warranty**	
Parts Replaced			YES	NO

Date		Equipment	
Serial No.		Model	
Repair Reason			

REPAIR DETAILS/ COST

Repaired by			**Warranty**	
Parts Replaced			YES	NO

FARM EXPENSES

Year

Balance Brought Forward:

Date	Description	Merchant	Qty	Cost Per Unit	Total Cost
		Subtotals:			

FARM EXPENSES

Year   Balance Brought Forward:

Date	Description	Merchant	Qty	Cost Per Unit	Total Cost
		Subtotals:			

Page 59

FARM EXPENSES

Year

Balance Brought Forward:

Date	Description	Merchant	Qty	Cost Per Unit	Total Cost
		Subtotals:			

FARM EXPENSES

Year

Balance Brought Forward:

Date	Description	Merchant	Qty	Cost Per Unit	Total Cost
		Subtotals:			

FARM EXPENSES

Year

Balance Brought Forward:

Date	Description	Merchant	Qty	Cost Per Unit	Total Cost
	Subtotals:				

FARM EXPENSES

Year

Balance Brought Forward:

Date	Description	Merchant	Qty	Cost Per Unit	Total Cost
	Subtotals:				

FARM EXPENSES

Year

Balance Brought Forward:

Date	Description	Merchant	Qty	Cost Per Unit	Total Cost
	Subtotals:				

FARM EXPENSES

Year

Balance Brought Forward:

Date	Description	Merchant	Qty	Cost Per Unit	Total Cost
		Subtotals:			

FARM EXPENSES

Year

Balance Brought Forward:

Date	Description	Merchant	Qty	Cost Per Unit	Total Cost
		Subtotals:			

FARM EXPENSES

Year

Balance Brought Forward:

Date	Description	Merchant	Qty	Cost Per Unit	Total Cost
			Subtotals:		

Page 67

FARM EXPENSES

Year

Balance Brought Forward:

Date	Description	Merchant	Qty	Cost Per Unit	Total Cost
		Subtotals:			

FARM EXPENSES

Year

Balance Brought Forward:

Date	Description	Merchant	Qty	Cost Per Unit	Total Cost
		Subtotals:			

Page 69

FARM EXPENSES

Year

Balance Brought Forward:

Date	Description	Merchant	Qty	Cost Per Unit	Total Cost
		Subtotals:			

FARM EXPENSES

Year

Balance Brought Forward:

Date	Description	Merchant	Qty	Cost Per Unit	Total Cost
		Subtotals:			

FARM EXPENSES

Year

Balance Brought Forward:

Date	Description	Merchant	Qty	Cost Per Unit	Total Cost
	Subtotals:				

FARM EXPENSES

Year

Balance Brought Forward:

Date	Description	Merchant	Qty	Cost Per Unit	Total Cost
	Subtotals:				

FARM EXPENSES

Year

Balance Brought Forward:

Date	Description	Merchant	Qty	Cost Per Unit	Total Cost
Subtotals:					

FARM EXPENSES

Year

Balance Brought Forward:

Date	Description	Merchant	Qty	Cost Per Unit	Total Cost
	Subtotals:				

Page 75

FARM EXPENSES

Year   Balance Brought Forward:

Date	Description	Merchant	Qty	Cost Per Unit	Total Cost
		Subtotals:			

FARM EXPENSES

Year

Balance Brought Forward:

Date	Description	Merchant	Qty	Cost Per Unit	Total Cost
			Subtotals:		

FARM INCOME

Year

Balance Brought Forward:

Date	Description	Buyer	Qty	Cost Per Unit	Total Cost
		Subtotals:			

Page 78

FARM INCOME

Year		Balance Brought Forward:			
Date	Description	Buyer	Qty	Cost Per Unit	Total Cost
		Subtotals:			

FARM INCOME

Year		Balance Brought Forward:			
Date	Description	Buyer	Qty	Cost Per Unit	Total Cost
		Subtotals:			

FARM INCOME

Year		Balance Brought Forward:			
Date	Description	Buyer	Qty	Cost Per Unit	Total Cost
			Subtotals:		

FARM INCOME

Year			Balance Brought Forward:			

Date	Description	Buyer	Qty	Cost Per Unit	Total Cost
		Subtotals:			

Page 82

FARM INCOME

Year

Balance Brought Forward:

Date	Description	Buyer	Qty	Cost Per Unit	Total Cost
		Subtotals:			

FARM INCOME

Year			Balance Brought Forward:			

Date	Description	Buyer	Qty	Cost Per Unit	Total Cost
		Subtotals:			

FARM INCOME

Year

Balance Brought Forward:

Date	Description	Buyer	Qty	Cost Per Unit	Total Cost
		Subtotals:			

FARM INCOME

Year		Balance Brought Forward:			
Date	Description	Buyer	Qty	Cost Per Unit	Total Cost
		Subtotals:			

FARM INCOME

Year			Balance Brought Forward:		
Date	Description	Buyer	Qty	Cost Per Unit	Total Cost
		Subtotals:			

FARM INCOME

Year					
Balance Brought Forward:					
Date	Description	Buyer	Qty	Cost Per Unit	Total Cost
		Subtotals:			

FARM INCOME

Year			Balance Brought Forward:		
Date	Description	Buyer	Qty	Cost Per Unit	Total Cost
		Subtotals:			

FARM INCOME

Year

Balance Brought Forward:

Date	Description	Buyer	Qty	Cost Per Unit	Total Cost
			Subtotals:		

FARM INCOME

Year			Balance Brought Forward:		

Date	Description	Buyer	Qty	Cost Per Unit	Total Cost
		Subtotals:			

FARM INCOME

Year

Balance Brought Forward:

Date	Description	Buyer	Qty	Cost Per Unit	Total Cost
	Subtotals:				

FARM INCOME

Year

Balance Brought Forward:

Date	Description	Buyer	Qty	Cost Per Unit	Total Cost
		Subtotals:			

FARM INCOME

Year		Balance Brought Forward:			
Date	Description	Buyer	Qty	Cost Per Unit	Total Cost
		Subtotals:			

FARM INCOME

Year			Balance Brought Forward:		

Date	Description	Buyer	Qty	Cost Per Unit	Total Cost
		Subtotals:			

FARM INCOME

Year

Balance Brought Forward:

Date	Description	Buyer	Qty	Cost Per Unit	Total Cost
		Subtotals:			

Page 96

FARM INCOME

Year		Balance Brought Forward:			
Date	Description	Buyer	Qty	Cost Per Unit	Total Cost
		Subtotals:			

NOTES

NOTES

NOTES

NOTES

NOTES

NOTES

NOTES

NOTES

NOTES

NOTES

YEAR ....

JANUARY	FEBRUARY	MARCH
1	1	1
2	2	2
3	3	3
4	4	4
5	5	5
6	6	6
7	7	7
8	8	8
9	9	9
10	10	10
11	11	11
12	12	12
13	13	13
14	14	14
15	15	15
16	16	16
17	17	17
18	18	18
19	19	19
20	20	20
21	21	21
22	22	22
23	23	23
24	24	24
25	25	25
26	26	26
27	27	27
28	28	28
29	29	29
30		30
31		31

APRIL		MAY		JUNE	
1		1		1	
2		2		2	
3		3		3	
4		4		4	
5		5		5	
6		6		6	
7		7		7	
8		8		8	
9		9		9	
10		10		10	
11		11		11	
12		12		12	
13		13		13	
14		14		14	
15		15		15	
16		16		16	
17		17		17	
18		18		18	
19		19		19	
20		20		20	
21		21		21	
22		22		22	
23		23		23	
24		24		24	
25		25		25	
26		26		26	
27		27		27	
28		28		28	
29		29		29	
30		30		30	
		31			

YEAR ....

JULY	AUGUST	SEPTEMBER
1	1	1
2	2	2
3	3	3
4	4	4
5	5	5
6	6	6
7	7	7
8	8	8
9	9	9
10	10	10
11	11	11
12	12	12
13	13	13
14	14	14
15	15	15
16	16	16
17	17	17
18	18	18
19	19	19
20	20	20
21	21	21
22	22	22
23	23	23
24	24	24
25	25	25
26	26	26
27	27	27
28	28	28
29	29	29
30	30	30
31	31	

OCTOBER	NOVEMBER	DECEMBER
1	1	1
2	2	2
3	3	3
4	4	4
5	5	5
6	6	6
7	7	7
8	8	8
9	9	9
10	10	10
11	11	11
12	12	12
13	13	13
14	14	14
15	15	15
16	16	16
17	17	17
18	18	18
19	19	19
20	20	20
21	21	21
22	22	22
23	23	23
24	24	24
25	25	25
26	26	26
27	27	27
28	28	28
29	29	29
30	30	30
31		31

YEAR ....

JANUARY	FEBRUARY	MARCH
1	1	1
2	2	2
3	3	3
4	4	4
5	5	5
6	6	6
7	7	7
8	8	8
9	9	9
10	10	10
11	11	11
12	12	12
13	13	13
14	14	14
15	15	15
16	16	16
17	17	17
18	18	18
19	19	19
20	20	20
21	21	21
22	22	22
23	23	23
24	24	24
25	25	25
26	26	26
27	27	27
28	28	28
29	29	29
30		30
31		31

APRIL	MAY	JUNE
1	1	1
2	2	2
3	3	3
4	4	4
5	5	5
6	6	6
7	7	7
8	8	8
9	9	9
10	10	10
11	11	11
12	12	12
13	13	13
14	14	14
15	15	15
16	16	16
17	17	17
18	18	18
19	19	19
20	20	20
21	21	21
22	22	22
23	23	23
24	24	24
25	25	25
26	26	26
27	27	27
28	28	28
29	29	29
30	30	30
	31	

YEAR ....

JULY		AUGUST		SEPTEMBER	
1		1		1	
2		2		2	
3		3		3	
4		4		4	
5		5		5	
6		6		6	
7		7		7	
8		8		8	
9		9		9	
10		10		10	
11		11		11	
12		12		12	
13		13		13	
14		14		14	
15		15		15	
16		16		16	
17		17		17	
18		18		18	
19		19		19	
20		20		20	
21		21		21	
22		22		22	
23		23		23	
24		24		24	
25		25		25	
26		26		26	
27		27		27	
28		28		28	
29		29		29	
30		30		30	
31		31			

OCTOBER	NOVEMBER	DECEMBER
1	1	1
2	2	2
3	3	3
4	4	4
5	5	5
6	6	6
7	7	7
8	8	8
9	9	9
10	10	10
11	11	11
12	12	12
13	13	13
14	14	14
15	15	15
16	16	16
17	17	17
18	18	18
19	19	19
20	20	20
21	21	21
22	22	22
23	23	23
24	24	24
25	25	25
26	26	26
27	27	27
28	28	28
29	29	29
30	30	30
31		31

Made in the USA
Monee, IL
23 March 2022